Helping Children See Jesus

ISBN: 978-1-64104-029-7

Prophets to God's People

*Old Testament Volume 24:
Kings, Chronicles, Minor Prophets Part 2*

Authors: Katherine E. Hershey (Kings & Chronicles)
Gertrude Landis (Minor Prophets)
Illustrator: Vernon Henkel
Computer Graphic Artist: Kristen Hall
Page Layout: Morgan Melton, Patricia Pope

© 2018 Bible Visuals International
PO Box 153, Akron, PA 17501-0153
Phone: (717) 859-1131
www.biblevisuals.org

All rights reserved. No part of this publication may be reproduced, stored in a retrieval system or transmitted in any form by any means, electronic, mechanical, photocopy, recording or otherwise, without the prior permission of the publisher, except as provided by USA copyright law.

RELATED ITEMS

To access related items (such as activities, memory verse posters and translated texts) please visit our web store at www.biblevisuals.org and enter 2024 at the top right of the web page. You may need to reduce the zoom setting to get the search box.

FREE TEXT DOWNLOAD

To obtain a FREE printable copy of the English teaching text (PDF format) under Product Format, please scroll down and select Extra–PDF Teacher Text Download. Then under Language select English before clicking the ADD TO CART button to place in your shopping cart. Other languages are available at an additional cost from the Language menu. When checking out, use coupon code XTACSV17 at checkout and click on Apply Coupon to receive the discount on the English text.

"As I live, says the Lord GOD, I have no pleasure in the death of the wicked; but that the wicked turn from his way and live."

Ezekiel 33:11a

© Bible Visuals International Inc

Lesson 1
ELIJAH, THE TRUE PROPHET

NOTE TO THE TEACHER

Prophecy is telling the message of God to man. Sometimes it tells what will happen in the future. More often it speaks of correction for God's people in the present. Prophets were chosen by God to be His messengers. Many times God's people accepted the prophetic messages. Too often they refused to listen to the prophets. For this, they suffered.

Biblical prophets apparently studied with other prophets who taught them. (See 2 Kings 2:3, 5, 16-18.) They would have learned how to hear and recognize God's voice. They had to know how to speak His message. To deliver God's prophecy at exactly the right time was very important.

In this and the two following volumes, God's prophets are featured. A fascinating study is ahead for you and your class!

Elijah (of the city of Tishbe) is a particularly interesting prophet. He could speak with fearsome authority and stand firm. But sometimes he prophesied, then ran far away and hid. And he ran long distances! Once he went 30 miles (48 kilometers) from Samaria to the Brook Cherith. From Cherith he went almost 90 miles (144 kilometers) to Zarephath to be fed. Later he spoke God's message to Ahab. When he ran form King Ahab, he went (to Beersheba and finally Horeb) more than 200 miles (320 kilometers)! Remember, there were no bicycles, no cars, and no buses when Elijah lived. Depending upon the age of your students, use back cover map to show places named.

When Elijah prophesied there would be no rain, there was none "for three-and-one-half years." (See Luke 4:25: James 5:17.) Ravens are known for *not* feeding their baby birds. (See Job 38:41; Psalm 147:9.) Yet ravens fed the exhausted, hungry Elijah. Such are the miracles of our loving Lord! Teacher, make the Bible live to your students!

Scripture to be studied: 1 Kings 16:30-33; 17:1-16; 18:1-19:3a; 21:1-25; Deuteronomy 11:16-17a

The *aim* of the lesson: To challenge students to know God's Word and obey it.

What your students should *know*: That because God loves His people, He sent prophets to lead them to repent.

What your students should *feel*: A desire to turn from sin and live to please God.

What your students should *do*: Listen to God's Word and obey His will.

Lesson outline (for the teacher's and students' notebooks):

1. God's punishment for idolatry (1 Kings 16:30-33; Deuteronomy 11:16-17a;1 Kings 17:1; 18:1-2).
2. God's provision for Elijah (1 Kings 17:2-16; 18:7-18).
3. God's power over Baal (1 Kings 18:19-19:3a, 16b).
4. God's pronouncement of judgment (1 Kings 21:1-25).

The verse to be memorized:

As I live, says the Lord GOD, I have no pleasure in the death of the wicked; but that the wicked turn from his way and live. (Ezekiel 33:11a)

THE LESSON

Have you ever heard someone say, "There will be rain tomorrow"? Maybe he said, "Day after tomorrow will be cold and windy." And perhaps he was exactly right. Or he may have been quite wrong.

Did you ever hear this: "There cannot be any rain until *I say* it will rain"? (No!) In the long ago, one man did say this. We shall learn about him today. Listen!

1. GOD'S PUNISHMENT FOR IDOLATRY
1 Kings 16:30-33; Deuteronomy 11:16-17a; 1 Kings 17:1; 18:1-2

King Ahab was ruling over Israel, the Northern Kingdom. Ahab married Jezebel. Jezebel came from Sidon, a land of idol-worshipers. (Show Sidon on back cover map.) Her father was king of those idol-worshipers. He would have demanded, "My daughter cannot marry Ahab. Never! Not unless he lets her take our gods (idols) into Israel!"

King Ahab knew God had forbidden His people to marry idol-worshipers. (See Deuteronomy 7:3-4.) But Ahab didn't care about God. He would not listen to Him–nor obey Him! So Jezebel, the idol-worshiper, became Queen Jezebel of the Northern Kingdom. And King Ahab built a temple with an altar for her gods. There he and she together worshiped idols made by men's hands. Ahab even let Jezebel teach God's people how to worship idols. So God was very angry with the king and queen–and with His people.

Then one day a man of God stomped into the palace. Sternly he announced to King Ahab: "As truly as the Lord, the God of Israel (whom I serve), lives, there will be no rain for the next few years–not until I say so!" He disappeared as quickly as he had come!

Who was this man? Does anyone have the right to say this? (Let students discuss.) The man who said "No rain until *I* say so," was Elijah. Elijah was a true prophet–a man who spoke for the living God. Elijah spent much time learning God's commands. When Elijah had heard about Ahab and Jezebel, he was distressed. The kings of God's people should help them love and worship God. But Ahab and Jezebel were causing the Israelites to forget God. God Himself had told Elijah what to prophesy to King Ahab. Would Elijah have been afraid of the king? Probably. But Elijah remembered God's awful punishment for idol-worship. He had carefully studied God's commandments.

Show Illustration #1

Elijah understood God's command: "If you turn away from Me and worship other gods . . . My anger will burn against you. I shall shut up the heavens so it will not rain. Crops will not grow. You will starve to death." (See Deuteronomy 11:16-17; 28:14, 23-24.) Elijah had to obey God and warn the king. So he had made his severe announcement: "There will not be dew or rain until I say so!" And immediately Elijah had disappeared!

The king and queen understood this was a message from God. But they cared neither for God nor His message. So they ignored God's prophet.

Do you ever ignore God or refuse to do what He says? Perhaps you disobeyed your parents. If you know God's Word, He could remind you of this verse: "Children, obey your parents." (See Ephesians 6:11. *Teacher:* Use a verse here which applies to your age group. For example, see Ephesians 6:4; 6:5; or 6:9.) What do you do about this? Do you listen–and obey? Or do you ignore God's Word as the king and queen did?

2. GOD'S PROVISION FOR ELIJAH
1 Kings 17:2-16; 18:7-18

Weeks and months passed. And, exactly as God had warned through Elijah, it did not rain. The king and queen began to worry. "Where, oh where is Elijah?" they wondered. King Ahab thought, *How can I find him?*

The truth is, the king could not find the prophet. For God had sent Elijah far away-safe from the angry king. Do you think Elijah prayed that it would not rain? Indeed, he did! He prayed *earnestly*! (See James 5:17.)

At first, God hid Elijah in the mountains by a sparkling brook (Cherith). Big birds (ravens) brought him bread and meat both morning and evening. So God provided Elijah with plenty to drink and eat.

Sometime later, because there was no rain, there was no brook. Then God told Elijah, "Go to Zarephath of Sidon. I have told a widow there to give you all the food you need."

Elijah was terrified! God was sending him to Queen Jezebel's homeland [in Phoenicia]. Then he realized how wise God is. He thought: *Ahab and Jezebel will never think of looking for me there! They would never expect me to be in a land of idol-worshipers*!

Elijah trudged mile after mile. Finally, at the city gate [of Zarephath] Elijah saw a widow. He asked her, "May I please have a drink of water? And may I also have a bit of bread?"

Sadly the woman answered, "I am sorry. I have no bread. I have only a handful of meal and a bit of oil. I plan to mix it and bake bread for my son and me. After that is gone, we shall die." Because there had been no rain, there was no food.

Elijah told her, "Do not be afraid to make a bit of bread for me first. Then make bread for you and your son. The Lord God of Israel will provide for you. He will keep giving you oil and flour until it rains again."

Show Illustration #2

The woman believed Elijah. And she must have had faith in the living God of Heaven. So she made food for Elijah and for her family. Elijah stayed there a long time (nearly three years!). And everyone in the house always had enough to eat. There was a miraculous supply of flour in the jar and oil in the jug!

During the third year of famine, God spoke again to Elijah. "Go see King Ahab," the Lord said. "I am going to send rain." Until this time Elijah had been hiding from Ahab. King Ahab blamed Elijah for all the trouble because of no rain. Now Elijah trusted the Lord to take care of him.

Elijah soon stood before King Ahab. The king angrily asked, "Is that you, you troubler of Israel?"

"I'm not the one who is troubling Israel," Elijah answered. "You and your father's family are the troublemakers! You have turned from the commandments of the Lord. You have followed Baal." Baal was the name of the most important of Jezebel's idols. Baal was also the rain god. But Baal certainly had not made it rain!

3. GOD'S POWER OVER BAAL
1 Kings 18:19-19:3a, 16b

To King Ahab, Elijah announced, "We are going to prove who is the true God. Tell all the people of Israel to meet on Mount Carmel. Bring the 450 prophets of Baal." Think of that many prophets speaking for their god! The god Baal had eyes, but it could not see. It had ears, but it could not hear. It had a mouth but it could not speak. It was made by a man. So Baal never had any life in it. (See Psalm 115:4-8; Isaiah 44:9-20 [particularly observe Psalm 115:8; 135:18].) Elijah continued, "Queen Jezebel has 400 prophets of another idol. Bring them along, too."

King Ahab decided to test Elijah. He sent the message to the Israelite people: "Gather at Mount Carmel!" Hundreds and hundreds of people obeyed the king.

There, on the mountain, Elijah demanded, "Make up your mind! If the Lord is God, follow Him. If Baal is god, follow him." Elijah explained, "I am the only one of the Lord's prophets here. Baal has 450 prophets. We shall take two oxen. You prophets of Baal, choose one ox and cut it up. Then lay the pieces on the wood on the altar. But do not put any fire under it. Then call on Baal. Later I shall put the other ox on the altar and call on my God. Whichever one answers by sending fire, He is the true God."

"Good!" the people shouted. "That sounds fair enough."

Show Illustration #3

Baal's prophets cut their ox into pieces, placing all on the altar. They shouted, "O Baal, answer us!" There was no fire. Over and over again–morning until noon–they screamed. No answer. They jumped and danced on the altar. "O Baal, answer us!"

Elijah, taunting them, commanded, "Call louder! Perhaps he has gone on a trip. Maybe he is asleep. If so, wake him up!"

The prophets of Baal shouted louder. They cut themselves with knives. Finally, at three o'clock, Elijah stepped forward. (Three o'clock was the time to offer the evening sacrifice to God.) "Come here!" Elijah commanded. "Listen to me!"

Taking 12 large stones, Elijah quickly built an altar. He put wood on it and built a trench around it. He cut up the ox, placing it on the wood. Then he demanded, "Fill four (4) big jugs with water. Pour the water over the sacrifice." The crowd stared in amazement. "Do it again!" Elijah ordered. Another time he called, "Do it again!" The ox, the wood, the altar–all were dripping wet. The trench overflowed. There would be no possibility of idolaters claiming the fire happened by chance!

Then Elijah prayed, "O Lord, . . . let it be known today that You are God in Israel. Help the people to know that I am Your servant. I have done all this at Your command. Answer me, O Lord, so the people will know that You, O Lord, are God. Turn their hearts back to You again."

Immediately fire fell from Heaven. It burned up the sacrifice, the wood, the altar, the soil. It even licked up the water in the trench!

Amazed, the crowd fell with their faces to the ground. They confessed, "The Lord–He is God! The Lord–He is God!"

Having seen God's wonderful miracle, these Israelites turned from idol-worship to Him.

The people prayed. But King Ahab didn't pray. Nor did Baal's prophets pray. Then Elijah commanded, "Grab every one of the prophets of Baal!" And that night all those prophets lay dead!

Again Elijah prayed. Then God sent the rain. Oh, how it rained!

Even so, the king and queen continued as wicked as ever. Jezebel was so angry, she tried to kill Elijah. He ran for his life and God helped him get far, far away. There he prayed, "I have had enough, Lord. Take my life."

Would King Ahab or anyone else ever again see Elijah?

4. GOD'S PRONOUNCEMENT OF JUDGMENT
1 Kings 21:1-25

Years later, King Ahab wanted the vineyard which belonged to his neighbor, Naboth. Wanting for oneself what belongs to another, is coveting–a sin God hates. (See Exodus 20:17.) Because of a certain law of God, Naboth could not sell his land. This made Ahab so angry he went to bed and refused to eat. When Queen Jezebel learned why Ahab was pouting, she was furious! So she had Naboth stoned to death. Then King Ahab took Naboth's vineyard for himself and Elijah saw him there.

Ahab panicked. "You've found me, O my enemy!" Ahab exclaimed.

Elijah's answer was serious. "I have found you because you have sold yourself to do evil. I have bad news for you, O King." Elijah's prophecy was frightening: "God is going to bring tragedy on you and your family. All your sons and grandsons will be killed. The dogs will lick your blood where they licked Naboth's blood. And, King Ahab, the Lord says, 'The dogs will eat Jezebel's body beside the city wall.'" (*Teacher:* Quote the verse to be memorized, Ezekiel 33:11.)

Show Illustration #4

And so it was. Jezebel died exactly as God had said. (See Hebrews 10:31.)

Surely you are not as wicked as Ahab and Jezebel. But we all do wrong at times. Doing wrong is sin. Even one sin separates us from God. God is perfect. He is holy–without any sin at all. We sin when we want something which belongs to someone else. This is coveting–a sin God hates. We may love something or someone more than God. This is the sin of idolatry. We may lie, cheat or pout. Anything wrong is sin, and God punishes sin. But God loves us. He gave His Son, the Lord Jesus, to take our punishment for sin. Have you received the Lord Jesus as your Saviour from sin? If not, will you remain after class so I can help you?

Have you already received the Lord Jesus? He is in your heart, but you have not been pleasing Him. Do not go on sinning. Confess your sin to God. Ask Him for His forgiveness. (See Proverbs 28:13; 1 John 1:9.) Turn around. Go God's way. Ask Him to help you live a life which pleases Him.

Lesson 2
FALSE PROPHETS

Scripture to be studied: 2 Chronicles 17:1-13; 18:1-19:4; 20:1-30

The *aim* of the lesson: To teach that God uses those who know and obey His will.

What your students should *know*: Today, God teaches His will through His Word.

What your students should *feel*: A desire to please God and be useful to Him.

What your students should *do*: Turn from any wrong friendships.

Lesson outline (for the teacher's and students' notebooks):

1. Ahab's false prophets (2 Chronicles 17:1-13; 18:1-6).
2. God's true prophet (2 Chronicles 18:1-27).
3. God controls all prophecies (2 Chronicles 18:28-19:4).
4. God speaks as He chooses (2 Chronicles 20:1-30).

The verse to be memorized:

As I live, says the Lord GOD, I have no pleasure in the death of the wicked; but that the wicked turn from his way and live. (Ezekiel 33:11a)

THE LESSON

Long, long ago, God chose for Himself a special people, the Jews. (Sometimes His people are called Hebrews or Israelites.) God gave the Jews a land in which to live. In time, they had a great temple in the city of Jerusalem. God taught the Jewish people exactly how to worship Him. He gave them good laws (rules) which they were to obey. Did King Ahab (about whom we studied in our last lesson) obey God's laws? (*No, he did

NOTE TO THE TEACHER

True prophets, like Elijah, spoke honestly for God. Their prophecies were not always believed. But every prediction they made came true. Not all prophets spoke as dramatically as Elijah. Some, like Micaiah, spoke simply but directly. There were also false prophets. Four hundred (400) of them agreed about one prophecy. Yet it was not fulfilled because their prophecy was not from God.

Wicked King Ahab (in Israel, the Northern Kingdom) did not believe God's prophets. He chose to listen to his 400 false prophets. As a result, King Ahab was killed in battle. And, true to Elijah's prophecy, dogs licked up his blood. (See 1 Kings 21:17-19; 22:38.)

not! Teacher: Have students discuss Ahab's disobedience.) Where did King Ahab rule? (*In Israel, the Northern Kingdom*) What was the Southern Kingdom called? (*Judah*)

1. AHAB'S FALSE PROPHETS
2 Chronicles 17:1-13; 18:1-6

Show Illustration #5A

Jehoshaphat became king of Judah, the Southern Kingdom, while Ahab ruled Israel. (Have students repeat Jehoshaphat's name several times.) When Jehoshaphat first became king of Judah, he truly honored God's Word. He even sent 16 important men to every city in his kingdom. They took God's Law Books (written on scrolls) and taught God's laws to the people. Those laws are now in the first five books of our Bible. (Genesis, Exodus, Leviticus, Numbers, Deuteronomy.)

King Jehoshaphat loved and honored God and His Word. So God honored him. He received so many wonderful gifts that he became rich and powerful. He had such a big army that no one fought against Judah.

Jehoshaphat wanted to be certain that wicked Ahab would not fight against Judah. So King Jehoshaphat went up to visit King Ahab.

Show Illustration #5B

King Ahab was so delighted, he held a big celebration for King Jehoshaphat.

Afterward King Ahab asked, "King Jehoshaphat, will you do me a favor? The city of Ramoth in Gilead (show back cover map) is part of my kingdom. But the Syrians have taken it from us. Will you go with me to fight the Syrians? Ramoth Gilead belongs to Israel and I want to get it back."

Jehoshaphat answered, "I am with you. My people are your people. We shall go to war with you. But first, let us ask the Lord. Then we shall know if we should really go to battle."

Jehoshaphat was promising that he and his soldiers would help wicked Ahab. Yet down deep inside, he did not feel quite right about it. He loved God and belonged to Him. He was not comfortable about joining the wicked Ahab.

Ahab agreed with talking to God. He called for his prophets–400 of them! He asked them, "Shall we or shall we not go to war against Ramorh Gilead?"

Immediately they shouted, "GO! The Lord will give you the victory!"

King Ahab was delighted; but King Jehoshaphat was not. He knew these 400 had not asked God about this. They were not true prophets. They simply said what wicked King Ahab wanted them to say.

2. GOD'S TRUE PROPHET
2 Chronicles 18:1-27

Jehoshaphat asked, "Is there a prophet of the Lord whom we can ask?"

Annoyed, King Ahab answered, "Oh, there is one man. But I hate him. He never prophesies anything good for me, only bad. His name is Micaiah." Turning to a messenger, Ahab muttered, "Get Micaiah."

When Ahab's messenger reached Micaiah, he whispered, "Listen! King Ahab's 400 prophets told him he will win over Ramoth Gilead. Be sure you agree with them. Give King Ahab the same message."

Micaiah answered, "I can tell him only what the Lord tells me."

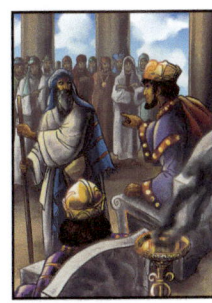

Show Illustration #6

The two kings, dressed in their royal robes, sat on thrones. When Micaiah came in, King Ahab spoke at once. "Shall we go to war against Ramoth Gilead or not?"

With a sing-song voice Micaiah answered, "Go and be victorious." Everyone knew Micaiah was mocking the other prophets.

Ahab shouted, "How often must I ask you to tell me the truth?"

Micaiah responded, "I saw all Israel scattered on the hills. They were like sheep without a shepherd."

Ahab turned to King Jehoshaphat saying, "See? I told you he never prophesies anything good about me, only bad!" Ahab understood the full meaning of Micaiah's prophecy. He, Ahab, would die because of the battle. The people (the "sheep") of Israel would be without a king ("shepherd").

King Ahab was wild with rage. "Throw Micaiah into prison!" he commanded. "Give him only bread and water until I return safely."

The true prophet, Micaiah, spoke softly. "If you return safely, the Lord has not spoken through me."

3. GOD CONTROLS ALL PROPHECIES
2 Chronicles 18:28-19:4

Amazingly, good King Jehoshaphat agreed to join wicked Ahab. Their armies would fight together. King Ahab decided he would not be killed. He would prove that Micaiah's prophecy was not true. Ahab thought, I *shall disguise myself*. He, the leader of Israel's army, would not wear his royal robe. Without it, the enemy would not recognize him.

To Jehoshaphat, Ahab said, "I shall disguise myself for the battle. But you go ahead and wear your kingly robe." Do you know what good King Jehoshaphar did? He obeyed wicked Ahab! He did. He really, truly did!

In Rarnoth Gilead the enemy army expected Ahab would wear his kingly robe. Their leader gave orders to those in charge of his 32 chariots. "Don't fight anyone except King Ahab of Israel. Get him! If he dies, his army will run away."

Show Illustration #7

Soon the chariot captains saw the man wearing a king's robe. "There's King Ahab!" they shouted, closing in on him.

King Jchoshaphar let out a war cry. Surprisingly, the charioteers stopped, turned about and wheeled away! Why did they not kill him? The Bible does not say. But we know that God had protected King Jehoshaphat.

Riding off, one enemy soldier set an arrow in his bow. He did not aim at anyone. He simply drew his bow and let the arrow fly. And it went right into King Ahab between the sections of his armor! Who could have guided that arrow through such a little opening? (*God.*) King Ahab commanded his charioteer, "Get me out of the fighting! I am wounded."

They took Ahab to the sidelines and propped him up in his chariot. From there, he watched the battle. Then, as the sun set, King Ahab died. His men took his chariot to a pool and washed it. (See 1 Kings 22:38.) And the dogs licked up his blood, exactly as Elijah had prophesied! (See 1 Kings 21:17-19.) King Ahab always went his own wicked way. For this the Lord was sad. Our verse (Ezekiel 33:11) tells us how God feels about the wicked. (*Teacher:* Have students quote the verse.)

King Jehoshaphat should have listened to Micaiah's prophecy. He should not have joined King Ahab. Yet God miraculously protected Jehoshaphat from being killed in battle. God, however, was displeased about his friendship with wicked Ahab. He sent Jehu, a prophet's son, to remind him of this. Jehu asked, "Was it right for you to help the wicked? Should you love those who hate God? God is not pleased about this. But God also sees the good you have done. You destroyed the idols in your land. And you set your heart on seeking God." After this, Jehoshaphat walked again in God's way. And he caused many people to return to the Lord.

4. GOD SPEAKS AS HE CHOOSES
2 Chronicles 20:1-30

One day some men came to King Jehoshaphat with frightening news. "A huge army is coming against us from the other side of the Dead Sea!" (Point to back cover map.) The enemy came from Ammon, Moab, Edom.

Jehoshaphat was terrified. Immediately he prayed to God. He sent the news throughout the kingdom. Crowds of people–men, women, children–rushed to the temple at Jerusalem. They came from every town to ask God for His help.

Jehoshaphat stood at the front of the temple and led them in prayer. "O Lord God . . . You rule over all the kingdoms of the nations. Power and might are in Your hand. No one can stand against You. We are in this land because You gave it to us." Jehoshaphat then talked to God about the enemy army. He closed his prayer saying, "O our God, judge the enemy. We have no power against this great army. Neither do we know what to do. But our eyes are upon You."

God did something wonderful and unusual. He caused a workman at the temple to give a message from God. The workman announced, "Listen to what God says to you. 'Do not be afraid of this great army. The battle is not yours, but God's. You will not have to fight. Stand still and see how God will save you. Do not be afraid nor discouraged. God will be with you.' "

King Jehoshaphat and all the people bowed down and worshiped the Lord.

The next day King Jehoshaphat encouraged the people to believe God's message. The king had his army ready. But what a strange-looking army it was!

Show Illustration #8

At the head of the army were many singers of the Lord. As Judah's army marched, the singers sang: "Give thanks to the Lord, for His love lasts forever." Oh, how they did sing! On the battlefield the army stood at attention while the singers sang.

The moment the enemy was ready to attack, something amazing happened. God caused the enemy soldiers to turn on each other. Instead of fighting against Judah, they destroyed their own men. Afterward the army of Judah saw only dead bodies lying on the ground. So they raced to the battlefield and gathered everything valuable. There were precious jewels, army equipment, clothing, and money. It took three days to collect it all! Finally everyone returned to Jerusalem. They met at the temple and praised God for His miraculous victory. Because King Jehoshaphat had trusted God, his people trusted Him also. And the Lord knows those who trust in Him. (See Nahum 1:7.)

After this, Judah again enjoyed peace. The Bible says, "The fear of God was on all the kingdoms" around them. They all knew that God had destroyed Judah's enemies.

During Bible times, God often spoke His messages to people through prophets. He used great men, like Elijah, and quiet men, like Micaiah. Once He entrusted His message to Jehu, the son of a prophet. And again He spoke through a workman at the temple. God gave His message as He pleased in Bible times.

Since God's Word, the Bible, was completed, prophets are not needed. God speaks to us now through His Word. We must read and obey its teachings.

From this study, we know God does not approve of our having evil friends. Do you have friends who laugh at God or hate Him? Do your friends disobey God's laws? What will you do about this? Will you obey God and give up those friendships? Will you talk to the Lord about this right now?

Lesson 3
FROM ONE PROPHET TO ANOTHER

NOTE TO THE TEACHER

Ever since the beginning of time, God has talked to his people. He Himself spoke personally to Adam, Eve, Noah, Moses, and others. Sometimes God gave His messages through angels. (See Luke 1:26-38; 2:8-14.) At times God spoke through angels who appeared as humans. (See Genesis 18:1-2.) Often God sent warnings through prophets, telling people of their sins.

Every prophecy a true prophet gave, had to come true. If it did not, the prophet had not given God's message. For this, he was to be put to death. (See Deuteronomy 18:20-22.)

The prophet Obadiah was sent to the Edomites, south of Judah. (See map.) The Edomites were descendants of Esau, Jacob's twin brother. (See Genesis 25:22-23, 30; 32:3; 36:1, 8-9; Numbers 20:14; Deuteronomy 23:7; Jeremiah 49:7-10.) Jacob (later named Israel) fathered the people of Israel and Judah. Esau and Jacob were enemies, even before they were born! (See Genesis 25:21-32.) When they were young men, Jacob cheated Esau twice (Genesis 25:27-34; 27:1-33). Years later, Esau finally forgave Jacob (Genesis 32:1-33:20). But his descendants, the Edomites, continued to be angry at Israel and Judah. (See Numbers 20:14-21.)

The reason for Obadiah's prophecy was this: Jerusalem (capital of Judah) had been invaded. And the people of Edom were delighted! They did not go to help their "brothers" in Judah. (See Obadiah 11-12.) Instead, the Edomites joined the invaders (verse 13). They even prevented the escape of the people of Judah (verse 14). For this, God said, Edom would be completely destroyed. (See verse 18; compare Jeremiah 49:7-22.) God's word came true. Edom and the Edomites disappeared almost 2,000 years ago! But the land of Israel and the Israelites exist today.

God continually warned His people through His prophets. Now, since the Bible was written, God speaks through it. He, the One who knows the end from the beginning, warns everyone. He longs for all people to turn to Him. May your students hear His voice as *you* teach.

Scriptures to be studied: 2 Kings 2:1-14; 3:4-24; 8:16-24; 2 Chronicles 21:1-7, 12-20; Obadiah 1-21

The *aim* of the lesson: To show that the true prophets' prophecies came directly from God.

What your students should *know*: What God says in His Word is absolutely rrue.

What your students should *feel*: A desire to study God's Word and obey it.

What your students should *do*: Pray for the Jews to turn to Christ the Lord.

Lesson outline (for the teacher's and students' notebooks):

1. Elisha prophesies (2 Kings 3:4-24).
2. Elijah prophesies (2 Chronicles 21:1-7, 12-20; 2 Kings 8:16-24).
3. Elijah is taken to Heaven (2 Kings 2:1-14).
4. Obadiah prophesies (Obadiah 1-21).

The verse to be memorized:

As I live, says the Lord GOD, I have no pleasure in the death of the wicked; but that the wicked turn from his way and live. (Ezekiel 33:11a)

THE LESSON

A teacher was telling her class about God's speaking to Moses. "The Lord said, 'This is what I want you to do.'"

Juan's hand shot up. "I wish God would talk to me so I could hear Him. If He did, I would surely do what He says."

His teacher wanted Juan to understand why God doesn't speak aloud today. "In the beginning God's Word was not written. God had to *tell* people exactly what He wanted them to know. Sometimes He Himself spoke directly from Heaven. Later He spoke through the prophets. Then God spoke through His Son, the Lord Jesus. (See Hebrews 1:1-2.) The Apostle Peter was one who heard God's voice. But he says God's written Word is even more important. (See 2 Peter 1:16-21.) Today we have the written Word, the Bible. And we can read it any time. If we think about what we are reading, God speaks to us. So we can hear Him every day–even many times a day! Would you like to hear God speak only once in a while? Or would you rather read every day what He says?"

(Encourage students to discuss their feelings about this. Help them to *want* to read God's Word.)

Israel's wicked King Ahab believed the prophecies of his 400 false prophets. He threw Micaiah, a true prophet, into prison. Why? (Have discussion of the previous lesson. Which prophecy came true? What happened to King Ahab?)

1. ELISHA PROPHESIES
2 Kings 3:4-24

Later, another king of Israel (the Northern Kingdom) had problems. The people of Moab (point to Moab on back cover map) owed a debt to Israel. Because their king refused to pay, war was declared. The king of Israel called his army together. Then he sent this word to King Jehoshaphat of Judah (the Southern Kingdom): "The king of Moab has rebelled against me. Will you fight with me against him?"

King Jehoshaphat answered, "My people and my horses are yours." So Judah and Israel joined forces.

"How shall we go?" the king of Israel asked.

King Jehoshaphat replied, "Through the Desert of Edom." (Show Edom on map.)

The king of Edom agreed to let Judah and Israel go through Edom. He even decided to join the battle! So the armies of Israel, Judah, and Edom marched against Moab. It was a rough march through the desert. After seven (7) hard days, they ran out of water. There was not a drop of water for the soldiers or the animals.

The king of Israel knew they were defeated. He asked, "Did God call us three (3) kings together so Moab can defeat us?" He was blaming God for their trouble!

King Jehoshaphat replied, "Is there a prophet of God here? If so, let us ask him what God says."

An officer had good news: "Elisha is down here. Elisha has been the servant of Elijah."

"The word of God is with him!" Jehoshaphat exclaimed.

So the three kings found the prophet Elisha and explained their problem. Elisha, seeing the king of Israel, was annoyed. The king of Israel wickedly worshiped idols. So Elisha refused to honor him. He said, "I respect Jehoshaphat, king of Judah." Turning to the king of Israel, Elisha spoke scornfully: "If it were not for Jehoshaphat, I would not even look at you!"

Elisha turned away. Finally he returned with God's message. Elisha announced, "The Lord says, 'Dig this valley full of ditches. There will be no wind or rain. But the valley will be filled with water–enough for you and your animals. This is easy for God. He will also give you victory over Moab.'"

All three armies rushed to dig ditches. The next morning every ditch was overflowing with water. The Lord had performed a miracle!

The soldiers of Moab, on their way to attack, were baffled. The water in the ditches looked blood-red in rhe morning sun. "Look at the blood!" they shouted. "The three armies must have fought and killed each other. Come! Let's take the loot!"

Show Illustration #9

The army of Moab raced into the valley. Immediately the soldiers of Israel burst out of hiding, attacked and defeated the Moabites. Israel was victorious because the prophet Elisha had given God's message. And God's message came true.

2. ELIJAH PROPHESIES
2 Chronicles 21:1-7, 12-20; 2 Kings 8:16-24

Later, King Jehoshaphat's oldest son became king of Judah. Jehoshaphat had been a good king. But his son, Jehoram, was very wicked. One of his first evil deeds was to kill his six brothers!

He soon heard from the Prophet Elijah. Usually Elijah spoke his prophecies. This time he wrote a fiery letter, saying: "This is what the Lord God of your father David says. 'You haven't followed the ways of the good kings of Judah. Instead, you've followed the ways of the wicked kings of Israel. You've made the people of Judah worship idols. You murdered your own brothers who were better than you. Now God is going to strike your nation. Your children, your wives, everything that is yours will be struck down. You yourself will die of a dreadful sickness.'"

Show Illustration #10

Everything God said to Jehoram through Elijah came true. Enemy nations looted the royal palace, grabbing everything. They carried away his sons and wives. Only one son was left–the youngest one. Let me tell you why God kept that son safe. Listen carefully! Jehoram and his children were of the family of King David. Jehoram was so wicked, his whole family could have been destroyed. But God had promised that David's family would continue. (*Teacher:* See Vol. 23 of this series, lesson #4.) This is what the Bible says: ". . . The Lord would not destroy the 'house' [family] of David. (See 2 Chronicles 21:7; compare 1 Kings 11:36.)

We may have forgotten God's promise to King David. But God never, never forgets! And He always keeps His promises. Elijah had warned the kings of Israel throughout his lifetime. This once, and by a letter, he had warned the king of Judah. All of Elijah's prophecies came true because he was God's true prophet.

3. ELIJAH IS TAKEN TO HEAVEN
2 Kings 2:1-14

One day the Prophets Elijah and Elisha were walking together. They were good friends. But Elisha understood that God would soon separate them. At the Jordan River, Elijah took off his coat. Rolling it up, he used it to strike the water. Immediately the river parted and Elijah and Elisha walked across on dry ground!

Turning to Elisha, Elijah asked, "What can I do for you before I leave you?"

"Please let me become a prophet like you," Elisha begged.

Elijah told him, "If you see me when I am taken from you, you will have what you asked."

Show Illustration #11

Suddenly a fiery chariot and horses separated Elijah and Elisha. And swish! . . . Elijah was caught up to God in a whirlwind!

Elisha cried to Elijah, "My father! My father!" Elisha runed and stared at the spot from which Elijah had disappeared. He picked up Elijah's coat. (Show front cover.) At the Jordan River, he asked, "Where is the Lord, the God of Elijah?" Then he struck the river with Elijah's coat. Immediately the river again parted and Elisha crossed on dry ground. He now understood that God would use him to replace Elijah.

The Lord certainly did use Elisha. He became the head of a school for prophets. (See 2 Kings 4:38-44; 6:1-7.) And Elisha performed many, many miracles–more than anyone except the Lord Jesus!

4. OBADIAH PROPHESIES
Obadiah 1-21

God used well-known prophets like Elijah and Elisha in Judah and Israel. He chose a little-known man, **Obadiah**, to prophesy in Edom. (Show Edom on back cover map.) **Obadiah** did not say much. (His entire prophecy is a total of only 21 Bible verses.) His prophecy, however, is very important.

The people of Edom (ancestors of Esau) should have been friendly to those in Judah and Israel (ancestors of Jacob). Their ancestors were brothers. But from the beginning, the people of Edom hated their relatives. Once, when the capital city, Jerusalem, was attacked, the Edomites were delighted. "Tear down the city!" they shouted. "Tear it down to its foundation!" (See Psalm 137:7.) This displeased the Lord.

Show Illustration #12

Through the Prophet **Obadiah**, God rebuked Edom. **Obadiah** spoke fiercely. "God says you are proud. You think you are safe because you are surrounded by mountains. You ask, 'who can bring me down to the ground?' God says, 'You may fly high like eagles. You may make your nest among the stars.' " Some Edomites lived in high caves up in the mountains. They felt perfectly safe. *No one can conquer us*, they thought. But God said, "I shall bring you down." (See Obadiah 3-4.) God hates pride (Proverbs 16:5).

Along with being proud, Edom acted wickedly. The Prophet **Obadiah** announced, "God says, 'You would not help Jerusalem when enemies attacked their city. (See Obadiah 11.) You, Edom, are their brothers (relatives). Yet you were glad to see their trouble (verse 12). You even crept into Jerusalem and stole from the people (verse 13). You set up roadblocks so they could not escape' " (verse 14).

God was angry at Edom. So **Obadiah** delivered God's warning: " 'As you have done to others, it will be done to you (verse 15) . . . The house of Esau will be straw. It will be destroyed by fire. There will be no survivors from the house of Esau.' The Lord has spoken" (verse 18).

God spoke, and it was so. Edom and all its people were totally destroyed.

Obadiah's short prophecy includes this warning from God: "The day of the Lord is near for all nations" (verse 15). God can send judgment at any time on any who rebel against Him. He will most certainly judge all nations when Jesus Christ returns and reigns on earth.

Was God pleased to destroy Edom? Will He be glad to punish all nations? Oh, no! Let's say our verse together: "As I live, says the Lord God, I have no pleasure in the death of the wicked, but that the wicked turn from his way and live" (Ezekiel 33:11).

Obadiah closed his short prophecy with good news from God. He tells the exact area in which God's people will live some day (verses 19-21). (*Teacher:* On back cover map, show the area. "The mountains of Esau" = Edom. From Edom up to Philistia including Jerusalem, Samaria; Gilead (on the east) and Zarephath (on the east). God's people are descendants of Jacob (Israel). The Lord had chosen them as a special people for Himself. Long ago they disobeyed God by worshiping idols. So He scattered them all over the world. Today God is waiting, eager for His people to turn to Christ. When they do, God's closing prophecy through **Obadiah** will come true; ". . . The kingdom will be the Lord's." The Lord Jesus Christ will then be King over all rhe earth.

Will you pray that many Israelite (Jewish) people will turn to the Lord Jesus Christ? When they receive Him their sins will be forgiven. Then they will be His forever. (*Teacher:* Close by having students pray for the salvation of Jewish people everywhere.)

Lesson 4
THE PURPOSE OF PROPHETS

Scripture to be studied: 2 Kings 6:8-7:20

The *aim* of the lesson: To show the purpose of prophets in Israel and Judah.

What your students should *know*: That God is always in control of everything.

What your students should *feel*: Confidence in God, knowing He is working for His people.

What your students should *do*: Decide to whom they can tell the Gospel.

Lesson outline (for the teacher's and students' notebooks):

1. A good prophet warns (2 Kings 6:8-15).
2. A good prophet comforts (2 Kings 6:16-23).
3. A good prophet is an example of faith (2 Kings 6:24-7:20).
4. A good prophet speaks for God

The verse to be memorized:

As I live, says the Lord GOD, I have no pleasure in the death of the wicked; but that the wicked turn from his way and live. (Ezekiel 33:11a)

> **NOTE TO THE TEACHER**
>
> This lesson emphasizes the purpose of the ministry of prophets. Their prophecies included messages of warning, comfort, examples of faith. Always they spoke for God.
>
> This series of lessons emphasizes the *kingdoms* of Israel and Judah. Therefore the accounts of Elisha's ministry are limited to the kings and the nations. God performed many other miracles through the Prophet Elisha. Study them for your own blessing, Teacher. Record them so you can occasionally share them with your students.
>
> Note how often Elisha is referred to as "a man of God." Teacher, do your students think of you as a man (or woman) of God? May it be so.

THE LESSON
1. A GOOD PROPHET WARNS
2 Kings 6:8-15

Trouble, trouble, trouble. The nation of Israel was in trouble. Why? Because the king and his people had turned from God to worship idols. So the nation of Israel had big trouble. Sometimes trouble causes people to return to the Lord. God's prophet, Elisha, wanted to help God's people. He gave this warning to the king of Israel: "The king of Syria is trying to capture you." (Point to Israel and Syria/Aram on back cover map.) "Be careful where you go, O king. The Syrians are watching you. They are out to get you."

Show Illustration #13

Time and again Elisha warned the king of Israel. "Do not go there! The Syrians are coming. Do not come here! The Syrians will get you! Stay away from such and such a place! Watch out for the Syrians!"

The Syrians always knew where the king of Israel was going. But each time they got to that place, he was gone. The king of Syria was furious. He called his officers together. "Which of you is a traitor?" he demanded. "Someone is telling our secrets to the king of Israel."

One officer answered, "None of us are traitors. We are not telling your secrets, O king!" Quietly he added, "Your problem is Elisha, the prophet of Israel. He tells Israel's king the words you whisper in your bedroom." Even the king's most private words were known to the prophet!

How did Elisha know the plans of the enemy king? God told him. God was caring for the people of Israel and their king. The Lord was protecting them from their enemy. Today He cares for us and protects us from our enemy, Satan.

The king of Syria was wild with rage. "Go find that prophet!" the king commanded. "I shall send men to capture him!" Since he had not caught the king, he would get the prophet.

The spies spotted Elisha and reported to the Syrian king: "Elisha is in the city of Dothan." (Point to Dothan on back cover map.)

At night, the Syrian king sent a small company of strong raiders with horses. He even sent chariots–enough to surround the city! That many, to capture *one* man! But that one man was a prophet of God. So the king of Syria was actually fighting God.

Early the next morning Elisha's servant saw the Syrians. He was terrified. He ran to Elisha crying, "Oh, my master! What shall we do?"

2. A GOOD PROPHET COMFORTS
2 Kings 6:16-23

"Do not be afraid," Elisha answered. "We have more with us than they have with them." The servant was baffled.

Elisha turned to God, praying. "O Lord, open my servant's eyes so he may see."

Show Illustration #14

God answered Elisha's prayer. The servant looked and saw the hillside full of horses and fiery chariots! God's angels were there protecting His two servants. (See Psalms 37:7; 91:11.) The Lord's unseen army outnumbered the Syrians!

The Syrian soldiers rushed to attack Elisha and his servant. Elisha stood still. Looking toward Heaven, he prayed: "Lord, strike these people with blindness." Immediately every enemy soldier was blind and bewildered! The soldiers groped about, not knowing what to do.

Elisha made an announcement to the Syrians. "This is not the road. This is not the city. Follow me! I shall lead you to the man you are looking for."

Elisha took command. "Line up!" Each soldier put a hand on the shoulder of the man ahead of him. "Forward march!" Elisha led the way. The soldiers stumbled along for 10 miles (16 kilometers) to Israel's capital in Samaria. There Elisha again prayed. "Lord, open the eyes of these men so they can see." The Lord instantly opened the eyes of the Syrian soldiers. And they saw the king of Israel–the very man they had so often tried to capture! To their great horror, they were helplessly captured by Israel's king.

The king of Israel was dazed. He had control of the Syrians without a battle! Turning to Elisha, he asked, "Shall I kill them?"

– 27 –

"No, do not kill them," Elisha replied. "Give them something to eat and drink and send them home." Imagine that! The king was to feed the enemy army and let them go. And that is exactly what the king did. He prepared a "great feast" for the Syrian soldiers. When they finished eating and drinking, the king sent them home. What do you suppose the king of Syria thought when he heard all this? (Let students discuss.) Would he decide never again to war against Israel?

For Israel, the good news was this: the Syrian raiding bands stopped attacking Israel. But there would be bad news. Listen!

3. A GOOD PROPHET IS AN EXAMPLE OF FAITH
2 Kings 6:24-7:20

Sometime later, the Israelites still had not turned from idols. So God allowed them to have more trouble.

Show Illustration #15

The king of Syria decided to capture Israel's capital city, Samaria. (Imagine! After Israel had treated his men so kindly!) This time he sent the entire Syrian army to surround the city. (Before, he had sent only a small company of soldiers–a raiding band.) Because Samaria was surrounded by Syrians, no one could leave or enter the city. There was no way of getting more food. The food in the city cost so much, only the rich could eat. (See 2 Kings 6:28-29.) Finally, all food was gone. And the people were starving. (The age of your group will determine what you tell about the dreadful famine.)

One day Israel's king was walking atop the city wall. From it, he could look down on his people in Samaria. A woman cried to him, "Help me, O King!"

"How can I help you?" the king asked bitterly. "I have no food anywhere. What is the matter?" When she told him her awful problem (see 2 Kings 6:28-29), the king was furious. He shouted, "I shall have Elisha beheaded this very day!"

The king blamed Elisha for Israel's trouble! The king should have known that Elisha was "a man of God." (See 2 Kings 6:6, 9, 15.) But he, the king had turned his back on God. He should have remembered the teachings of the Law of God. (See Deuteronomy 28:15, 49-53.) But he, proud king of Israel, had sinned against God's Law. Instead of worshiping God, he worshiped idols. He chose not to listen to the warnings of God through Elisha. So he planned to kill God's prophet! At once he sent a messenger to Elisha's house.

Elisha, in his house, was talking to some officials of the land. Just before the messenger came, Elisha said, "The king is planning to kill me today. Someone is on his way this minute. The king will come right after him."

Exactly what Elisha said would happen, did happen.

The king stomped in shouting, "Elisha, this famine is from the Lord! Why should I wait any longer for God to do something?"

Elisha interrupted the king. Sternly, he commanded, "Listen to the word of the Lord."

Show Illustration #16

Then, with a smile, Elisha prophesied: "Tomorrow there will be food. Flour and barley will be sold at the city gate. And everyone will be able to buy it."

Elisha had believed God would take care of His people. Now the Lord had given His promise through His prophet.

(*Teacher:* You may want to tell of the servant's unbelief and its result. See 2 Kings 7:2, 17-20.)

At this rime, four men with leprosy lived outside Samaria's city gate. (Leprosy was a dreadful sickness. So people with leprosy had to live outside the city.) These four could see the Syrian army camped nearby. The men, sick with leprosy, were discouraged. "Why do we sit here until we die?" one asked.

Another replied, "If we could go into the city, it would not help. There is no food there and we would starve."

One man had an idea. "If we go into the city, we shall die. If we stay here, we shall die. So let's go to the camp of the Syrian soldiers. We can surrender to them. If they spare us, we shall live. If they kill us, then we die." It was a daring plan. But they all agreed. They limped to the Syrian camp, arriving after dark. Everything was quiet. Not a soldier was in sight. The men stumbled into one empty tent and found food–lots of it. They gulped down every bit. Then they hurried to another tent. There they found clothing, silver, gold, and more food. In one tent after another they helped themselves. Not one Syrian soldier was in sight!

Why had the Syrian army disappeared? The Bible tells us. The Syrians had heard loud noises coming from the north and the south. There were sounds of chariots, horses, and great armies. The rumbling of chariot wheels and the pounding of horses' hoofs terrified the Syrians. To one another they screamed, "The king of Israel has hired other nations to attack us!" Wildly the Syrians raced towards their homeland, leaving everything behind. But there were no armies coming. God had simply sent the *sound* of armies. The Lord caused the Syrian army to hear the *sounds*. God had worked for Israel!

The men with leprosy realized there was more food than they could use. So they began hiding what they found. Suddenly they felt guilty. "We are not doing right," they agreed. "This is a day of good news. And we are keeping it to ourselves. The people in Samaria must hear about all this food." So they hurried to Samaria. They called out to the gatekeeper: "We have found food, clothing, silver, gold!"

The gatekeeper rushed the news to Israel's king. The next morning the people heard this great announcement: "There is food–food for everyone!" The people raced to the deserted army camp and gathered all they needed. There was so much extra food, it was brought to the city gate. There, everyone was able to buy it–exactly as Elisha had prophesied. God had provided for His people because the four men told the news.

4. A GOOD PROPHET SPEAKS FOR GOD

The prophet Elisha sometimes prophesied good news to those in trouble. His teacher, Elijah, was a prophet through whom God often prophesied bad news. True prophets gave God's message, whether the news was good or bad. Even when the prophecy was bad news, God was working for His own people. He allowed trouble so they would turn to Him.

God is not pleased to punish the wicked. He wants them to turn to Him, away from their evil ways. Let us say our verse together. (Ezekiel 33:11.)

In the long ago, the Lord used prophets to tell His message. But there are no prophets today. Their work was finished after the Bible was written. Today God allows you and me to tell His Word to others.

The four with leprosy could have kept quiet about all they found. If they had done so, would they have felt happy? Contented? Selfish? (*Teacher:* Encourage discussion.)

Show Illustration #17

You have heard the good news of the Gospel: "Christ died for our sins (*Teacher:* point to cross in illustration) . . . He was buried . . . He rose again the third day" (1 Corinthians 15:3-4). Have you told this good news to others? Have you explained how you turned to the Lord Jesus Christ?

Decide now with whom you will share God's good news this week.

(*Teacher:* Close with earnest prayer that your students will witness eagerly. Remember! They will follow *your* example. If you have unsaved in your group, encourage them to remain after class. When all is quiet, explain to them God's plan of salvation.)

www.ingramcontent.com/pod-product-compliance
Lightning Source LLC
Chambersburg PA
CBHW060801090426
42736CB00002B/120